Auntie's Knitting a Baby

Auntie's Knitting a Baby

By Lois Simmie

ILLUSTRATED BY ANNE SIMMIE

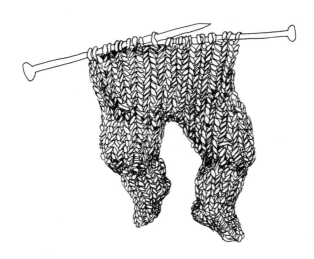

ORCHARD BOOKS

A DIVISION OF FRANKLIN WATTS, INC.
NEW YORK

Orchard Books
A division of Franklin Watts, Inc.
387 Park Avenue South
New York, New York 10016

Originally published in Canada by Western Prairie Books.
Printed in the United States of America.

10   9   8   7   6   5   4   3   2   1

Library of Congress Cataloging-in-Publication Data
Simmie, Lois, 1932–   Auntie's knitting a baby.
Summary: A collection of humorous poems covering such
subjects as an attic fanatic, a brother who is afraid of germs, and a
woman who knits strangely shaped baby clothes.   1. Children's
poetry, Canadian. [1. Humorous poetry. 2. Canadian poetry]
I. Simmie, Anne, 1956–   ill. II. Title.
PR9199.3.S5185A96   1988   811'.54   88-42546
ISBN 0-531-05762-3
ISBN 0-531-08362-4 (lib. bdg.)

This book is for Odette, and Daniel, and for all of the old children everywhere. It is also for Auntie Eva, who really is a terrible knitter.

The author wishes to thank Anne Szumigalski for her invaluable editorial assistance.

CONTENTS

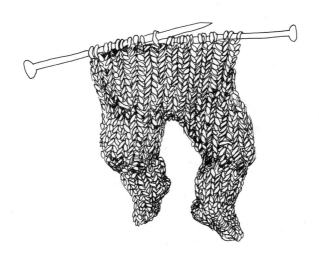

ATTIC FANATIC

As I lie in my bed
Things scratch overhead,
They rustle and scrabble and scurry;
And I've got a feeling
That over the ceiling
Are things that are scaly and furry.

Dad says they're just bats,
I see pythons and rats,
Grizzlies and starved alligators;
Dragony things
With claws, fangs and wings . . .

OH PLEASE CALL THE EXTERMINATOR!!!!!!!

AUNTIE #1

Auntie's knitting a baby bonnet
That looks like the lid of a pot;
If Auntie's baby fits that hat
It's not going to look so hot.

WISHING

I wish that my hair had some curly
And my clothes had some frilly and swirly;
That my nose wasn't runny
And my ears weren't funny,
That my name wasn't Alvina Shirley.

I wish that my room had some neat,
And my legs didn't have so much feet;
That my father could cook,
That my line had a hook,
That my red skirt had more than one pleat.

I wish that my cat had a tail,
I wish that my school had no fail;
That my yard had a pool
And my toad had a stool,
That my brother was locked up in jail.

I wish that my eyes were true blue
And my tooth wasn't loose when I chew;
That my bike had a chain,
That my head had a brain,

I wish I was somebody new.

WINNIE

Don't teeter totter with Winnie,
She'll trick you every time;
While you're up in the air
Like a bird or a stair
She jumps off and you fall on your spine.

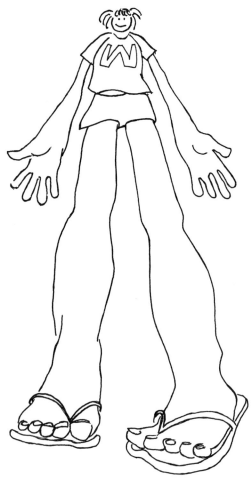

Like a hot potato she drops you,
You hit the ground with a SPLAT!
Your legs are broke
And you've had a stroke
And you don't have a clue where you're at.

No, don't teeter totter with Winnie,
If you want to grow up to be large;
For Winnie's as mean
As a guillotine
And as big as an ocean barge.

Kids teeter totter with Winnie
Who are dopey and don't have a clue;
They end up in a basket
Or maybe a casket,
Looking like yesterday's stew.

Oh, don't teeter totter with Winnie,
For Winnie's as mean as a snake;
She'll drop you as flat
As a butter pat
And gather you up with the rake.

AUNTIE #2

Auntie's knitting a baby bonnet
That looks like an airport wind sock;
If Auntie's baby fits that hat
She's in for a terrible shock.

POINT OF VIEW

Grandfather Gilly stands on his head
Wherever he takes the notion;
In the street, in the park,
In the daylight or dark,
In Regina. Or Moose Jaw. Or Cochin.

My mother and grandma have asked him to stop,
People think he is crazy, they say;
He replies, "I don't care
If they stand and they stare,
It undoubtedly brightens their day."

So Grandfather Gilly keeps standing around
With his toes in the air and his nose on the ground;
Though they call him unfit
He simply won't quit,
For he likes the world best upside down.

GERMS

My brother is afraid of germs,
He says they're everywhere . . .
On cats and mats and thermostats,
In the water. In the air.

He always laughs with his mouth shut
In case some germs get in;
He eats bananas all the time,
They're safe inside the skin.

He wears gloves and a surgical mask
Everywhere he goes;
He boils his knife and fork and plate,
And flushes toilets with his toes.

He scrubs his hands with Comet
And won't let anyone kiss him;
One of these days they'll take him away,
Nobody's going to miss him.

A SNAKE STORY

I saw a snake that looked so sad
I asked him why he felt so bad;
He looked me up and looked me down
And then he looked me all around . . .
He curled his neck around his head
And this is what he said:

"Oh say kind sir, you surely see
How sad you'd be if you were me;
Birds are pampered for their song,
Cats are stroked their nine lives long,
Dogs are petted and made friends of,
Snakes are simply to make ends of.

Bricks and bats and rocks they use,
You don't get used to such abuse;
'Stun it, hit it, kill it quick!
Get a stone and bring a stick!
Cut its tail off, it won't miss it,'
No one ever wants to kiss it.

'Kick it! Kill it!' they all shout,
'Knock the horrid thing about.'
Do they care that my bones ache?
Do they want to stroke a snake?
No one says 'what lovely creatures.'
No one says 'what noble features.'

So go ahead and kill me now,
I'm tired of living anyhow.
Goodnight, cruel world. Farewell. Goodbye."
He bowed his head and closed his eyes.
Just an old striped garter snake
Curled up by our garden rake.

I said, "you don't fill me with dread,
And I'd feel sad if you were dead.
You're beautiful," I said to him,
My mother called and I went in.
And when I went back out to play,
The spot was empty where he lay.

ANOTHER SNAKE STORY

I saw a snake go by today
Riding in a Chevrolet;

He was long and he was thin
And he didn't have a chin;

He had no chin, but what the heck,
He had lots and lots of neck.

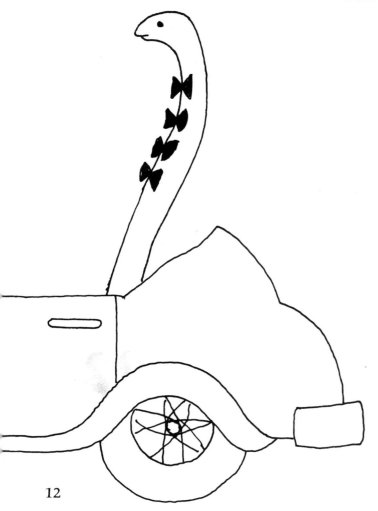

AUNTIE #3

Auntie's knitting a baby bonnet
That looks like an oriole's nest;
If Auntie's baby fits that hat
It's sure gonna feel depressed.

OUR CANARY

Our canary is dusty and cold and mad,
She sits around in a rage
Since we sucked her up in the vacuum hose
While cleaning out her cage.
Her feathers stayed behind in the bag
When we blew her out the end . . .

We're sending her off to Florida
Till her feathers grow in again.

JOSEPHINE CALICO
(for my cat, Josie)

My cat is white and orange and black
And pink and golden-green;
If you see a cat that looks like that,
Her name is Josephine.
Her coat is a glossy orange and black,
Her paws and whiskers are white,
The pupils that float in her shiny eyes
Are as black as a starry night.
Her eyes are the golden-green of leaves
When they are very young,
The pink of a peony's something like
Her rough and gentle tongue.
You are the luckiest kid around
And you already know it, I think,
If your cat is black and orange and white
And gold and green and pink.

THE KITCHEN WITCH

My mother has a kitchen witch
Hanging from the light,
She's riding on a broomstick,
Her hair is wild and white;
Her boots are black, her nose is long,
Her eyes are dark and squinty;
Her skirt is blue and billowy,
Her shawl is dark and printy.

She's supposed to be a good-luck witch
For gravies and cakes and pies;
Everybody thinks it's cute
But it's only a disguise.

I know about the kitchen witch
Hanging from the light,
And I'm the only one who knows
What she does at night . . .
When we're in bed and the lights are out
She flies around the house,
From room to room on her stiff brown broom,
Silent as a mouse.

Evil is always lurking
In her beady little eyes,
She planted a wart on the back of my hand,
It's grown to an awful size.
She killed the fish in my brother's tank,
He thought it was the ick;
Then he got pneumonia
And failed arithmetic.

With my head hidden under the blankets,
I heard her dry little laugh;
Well, that was the night she flew to the barn
And killed the newborn calf.
My mother's been trying not to smoke
But she's lighting up again;
The crops are bad and Dad's so sad,
Lightning got Uncle Ben.

Something really bad is coming,
And nobody will listen;
That witch just rides and rides and rides
And her black eyes glisten.

THE DREAM

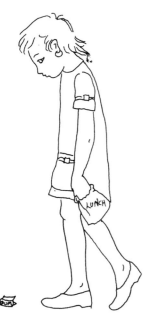

There's a dream I have about finding money,
I've had it a zillion times;
I'm walking along and there on the ground
Is a brand new shiny dime.
I pick it up and see some more
Half buried in the ground;
Dimes and quarters and silver dollars
Gleaming all around.
There's always more, and more, and more,
I know I am rich as a king;
I fill up my shirt and my scarf and shoes
And a rich person's song I sing.

"Oh, I am as rich as a king and a queen,
I will buy everything that I see;
Ponies and kittens and soft furry mittens,
A ring and a chimpanzee,
A playhouse, a bank and some fish in a tank,
A swimming pool, just for my folks,
An electric train and an aeroplane,
Pizza and candy and cokes."

But always before I get back home
To count up all that loot,
I wake up, remember it's just a dream
And I'm totally destitute.
Still, I keep on having that dream,
I know it must be a sign;
So I'm walking around with my nose to the ground
And a curvature in my spine.

MARY McBICKLE ONE

Mary McBickle choked on a pickle
And turned up her thin little toes;
Mary dying at dinner that way
Made Father feel quite indisposed.

HAUNTED

One summer day, down by the lake
I threw a stone at a little snake;
I only meant to scare him some
And to relieve the tedium.
It didn't just scare him, it killed him dead,
Now his thin little ghost comes each night to my bed.

He comes every night and he gives me no rest,
He curls on my pillow, he lies on my chest;
He wails in his little snake voice, so pathetic,
His little snake sobbings so soft and poetic . . .

"Oh, why did you kill me, you nasty big brute,
When I was so little, and helpless, and cute?
Now I'll never feel sun and I'll never eat fruit
Or talk to a newt, but you don't give a hoot,
With that horrid big rock you just put me away,
Now I'll haunt you and haunt you until you are grey."

He doesn't pay heed to my pitiful cries,
He just lies there and stares with his little snake eyes;
His tiny snake eyes, full of sorrow and spite,
His little snake body so see-through and white.

I can't tell my mother, I can't tell my dad
For I know I've been wicked, I know I've been bad;
With this weird little ghost I know I'll be cursed
Till I'm old or I'm dead, whichever comes first.

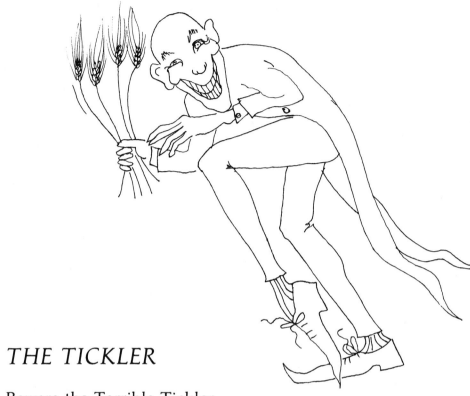

THE TICKLER

Beware the Terrible Tickler
With his fitted-out tickling kit;
If you don't run away he's coming today
To give you a tickling fit.

He uses a hummingbird feather
To tickle your mouth and your nose;
And a bouquet of bearded barley
To tickle your ten little toes.

He'll tickle your ears with a billy goat's beard,
Your nose with a pink parakeet;
He uses a bristly bottle brush
To tickle the soles of your feet.

He tickles your ribs ferociously,
Ignoring your pitiful cries;
The Terrible Tickler never stops,
Some delicate children have died.

He tickles and tickles and tickles
Till you can't tell the night from the day;
Then he packs up his fitted-out tickling kit
And merrily goes on his way.

AUNTIE #4

Auntie's knitting a baby bonnet
That looks like a butterfly net;
If Auntie's baby fits that hat
It's going to be hard to forget.

THE POET

Hurry hurry find a pencil,
Father's got a poem;
Run fast and get some paper,
Turn down the telephone.
When a poem comes on Dad
He's always lost the writing pad,
And if the poem gets away
Father mopes and sulks for days

So . . . . .

He writes in the dust beneath the bed,
He writes on Grandpa's shiny head,
He scribbles poems in the chimney soot
And once with lipstick on his foot.
So hurryhurry find the paper
Find the pencil and eraser,
It's a lot of bother being at home
When Father gets a poem.

THE INVENTOR

My mother's brother invents things,
He's been doing it for years,
Though he never makes any money
And his bills are in arrears.

He invents things in the basement,
He invents them night and day:
Artificial horns for cows,
Elephant repellent spray,

Winter boots for cattle,
Chocolate-scented air,
Pogo sticks for rabbits,
Spray-on underwear,

A machine to recycle cat hair
And one to recycle cats;
The basement's full of copper tubing,
Wires, pliers, rats and vats.

Sometimes he sets things on fire,
Sometimes he gets things exploding,
When Uncle doesn't come upstairs,
Auntie feels foreboding . . .

She knows he's creating a monster,
She's afraid he'll be finished it soon;
She wishes she'd gone with somebody else
When she went on her honeymoon.

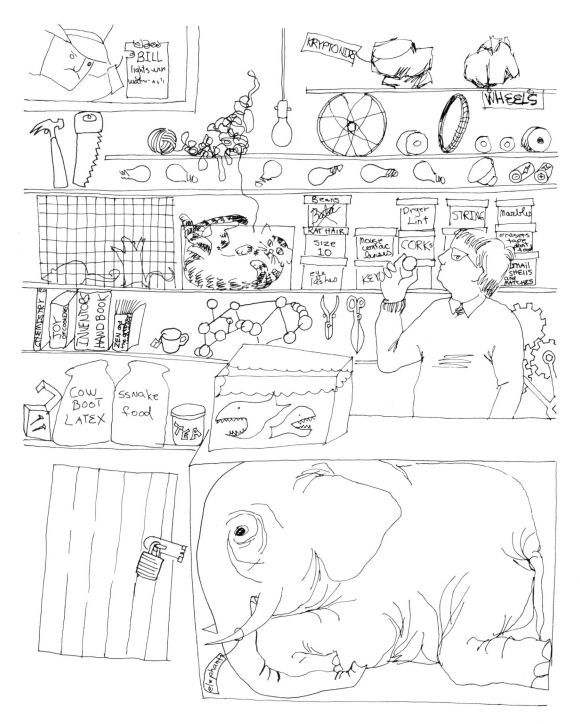

VAMPIRE POEM

If you think
Mosquito bites pain ya,
Be glad you don't live
In Transylvania.

MEAN

I wonder why
I feel so mean.
Was it something I ate?
Maybe a mean bean?

I just yelled at Mom,
Stuck my tongue out at Lee,
I'd pinch the baby
If no one could see.

He's lying there looking
So sweet and so nice,
While I'm full to the top
With sin and vice.

I just stepped on an ant,
I'm looking for more,
And some mud to track in
On Mom's clean floor.

I've been good for days,
At least fifteen;
And it sure feels good
To feel this mean.

MARY McBICKLE TWO

Mary McBickle choked on a pickle,
Screamed "I'm dying!" and promptly did;
"Just as well," her mother said,
"She might have been an invalid."

THE NEIGHBOURS

The neighbours are exciting to visit,
There's three of us and eleven of them;
The neighbours are exquisite to visit,
I was there last night and I'm going again.

Sammy has rabbits and Barry has pigeons,
Tammy has guppies and mice;
Their dog's having puppies, I hardly can wait
Gil ate a goldfish and said it was nice.

Simon is digging a hole to China,
He's worked on it all week long;
His father drove in from the alley last night
And stopped halfway to Hong Kong.

Jonathan's band is rocking
With the speakers amplifying;
The twins are covered with little red spots,
Jackie got smacked for lying.

The baby is getting her baby teeth,
Joshua's getting expelled;
The neighbours' father smokes a lot,
Their mother drinks muscatel.

Their mother is having a basement sale
The week before Hallowe'en;
She's sticking price tags on rabbits and kids
And looking kind of mean.

No one's going to buy them, I hope,
It just wouldn't be the same;
The neighbours are exquisite to visit
I was there last night and I'm going again.

31

AUNTIE #5

Auntie's knitting a baby bonnet
That looks like a hot air balloon;
When they tie that hat on the baby
It'll float right up to the moon.

DYING, MAYBE

Can't eat my porridge, can't swallow my toast,
Just looked in the mirror, I'm pale as a ghost;
I should stay at home today, snug in my bed,
They should keep me at home so I don't end up dead.

Oh Mother please tell me I don't have to go
Out in the dark and the cold and the snow;
It's minus nineteen out and cozy in here,
There's a pain in my stomach and maybe my ear.

You could put on my favourite Charlie Brown sheets,
And bring me my favourite munchies to eat;
Tomato soup on the green flowered tray,
Potato chips, ginger ale, just for today.

You could feel my poor forehead, rub my cold feet,
Wheel in the tv just for Sesame Street . . .
You could bring me my books, and my crayons, and cat,
You could sit by the bed with your coffee, and chat.

There's an ache in my ankle, or maybe my toe,
That's sure to get worse if you tell me to go;
What? You think I'm just faking? Just making a story?
Well, I'll die at my desk and then you'll be sorry.

NEET PEOPLE

The people of Neet have triangular feet
With a toe on each point, six in all;
They stand up like brooms
In the corners of rooms,
In foyers, and closets, and halls.

The people of Neet are quite fond of their feet
Which look something like pieces of pie;
And they're happy to stay
In the corners that way
For the people of Neet are all shy.

The corners in Neet are all filled up with feet
For they stand there from morning till night;
The people of Neet
Are all gentle and sweet
But they aren't especially bright.

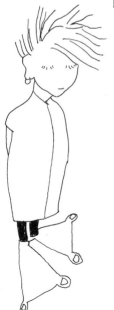

HEARTS

Everyone knows that the heart in your chest
Is all there's supposed to be;
So I worry a lot cause I've got a whole bunch
Beating inside of me.
I must be a medical miracle case,
I've got hearts all over the place.

There's one in each ear, I can hear them at night
When I'm lying still in my bed;
They thump in my pillow and keep me awake
Cause they're not sposed to be in my head.
Your head is supposed to be filled up with brain,
(Which is probably why I am going insane).

There's one in each jaw, or maybe there's not . . .
Those might be the ones in my ears . . .
The heart in my neck is the strongest of all,
I can feel it so plain and it's weird.
I've heard that a heart is as big as a fist
But I know it's not true cause there's two in my wrists.

How many is that now? I keep losing track,
You see why I can't get to sleep?
I just lie there and listen for thumps, beats and bumps,
It gives me the hollow-eyed creeps.
I keep finding new ones, there's more yet, I know,
I won't be surprised to find one in my toe.

I'm a nervous wreck, it shows in my face,
Hearts are thumping all over the place;
I can't play football, or hockey, or darts,
You have to take care when you're all full of hearts.

I WISH

I can't get to sleep, I'm feeling so bad,
Stan hit my nose and it bled;
Stanley's my friend, but today he's not,
The dog won't sleep on my bed.

Mom's in the kitchen yelling at Dad,
And I wish I could fly away;
Away in the dark with the wind and the stars,
And come back . . .

Another day.

MARCH

I'm waiting for spring and it's taking so long,
It's going to be winter forever;
I'm tired of snowballs and snowmen and snow,
Of freezing my nose and my fingers and toes,
I want to go barefoot, and smell a new rose,
But I know that it won't happen. Ever.

My mother and father are talking of gardens
And going to the lake when it's summer;
But there's snow in the garden and ice on the lake,
My feet are so cold they are starting to ache,
I'll *scream* if I see just one more snowflake,
And I just couldn't feel any glummer.

My skippping rope's rotting, my sandals are, too,
There's no such a feeling as hot;
There's ice on the swings and the slide and the roof,
Cold clumps of snow in my cuffs and my boots,
And I'm giving away my bathing suits,
For it's obvious God has forgot.

OUR MOLE

Where does he go, our mole?
The one who lives under the lawn.
Where does he go in winter?
The one who steals up at dawn
And steals my mother's flowers
To decorate his room,
Or toss a little salad
To nibble in the gloom.

Where does he go, our mole,
When everything's icy and cold?
Does he warm himself all winter
With a little lump of coal?
Does he sleep in a sleeping bag
Of softest dandelion fluff?

Mole, if you're still down there,
Somewhere . . .
I do hope you're warm enough.

MY DOG
(for Teddy)

Everyone says that my dog is old,
We've had him forever and ever;
But he's just the same as he's always been,
There's no change whatsoever.

Well, maybe he's got a few grey hairs
Around his mouth and his chin;
But when he runs after sticks and balls
He grins the same old grin.

He's just the same as he always was,
Though sometimes he moves kind of slow;
He still chases cats and squirrels and skunks,
And a lizard, once, down in Mexico.

It's nice when he sleeps on my feet at night,
As warm as an eiderdown;
And when I'm stretched out by the fireplace
He's the best kind of pillow around.

I can feel his heart just beating away,
It sounds even stronger than mine;
He just sleeps a bit more than he used to,
Since he fought with that porcupine.

He still rolls over and shakes a paw
Even though he thinks it's dumb;
But he trembles more than he used to
When thunder rolls like a drum.

He sits outside in the warm spring sun
And the wind puff-ruffles his ears;
My belly gets glad just looking at him,
Sad, too . . . and that's kind of queer.

He still comes to meet me after school.
He is lovely and warm to hold.
And he likes me better than anyone else,
No, my dog is *not* getting old.

ON THE MOUNTAIN OF MOUND

On the Mountain of Mound
Folks have feet that are round
With their toes going round in a ring;
They stand in wet holes
To cool off their soles,
They stand in wet holes and they sing:

"Oh, we are the luckiest
Creatures on earth
For we live on the Mountain of Mound,
Where the mud as it flows
Between thousands of toes
Gives a wonderfully musical sound.

Oh, we are the marvelous
Marvels of Mound
With the handsomest feet in the land,
And we know, yes we know,
Without telling us so,
That we round-footed creatures are grand."

They just stand there and sing
With their toes in a ring
And their voices all trembly and trilly;
They all looked contented
And slightly demented
And terribly, terribly silly.

MARY McBICKLE THREE

Mary McBickle choked on a pickle
And fell over dead as a nail;
Though they tickled her feet
With the tail of a beet
She would not either in or ex hale.

NINNY BIRD SKIPPING SONG

A silly little ninny bird
Sitting on a noodle
Was twittering a silly little
Ninny bird song.
Along came the cook
With his big wooden mallet
       !
Silly little ninny
Bird songs aren't long.

                Now

The cook
He is a-stirring
And the cook
He is a-singing
About ices
And spices
And dinner for ten

About oodles
Of strudel
And Ninnybird Noodles
And silly little ninny
Bird songs

              Amen

AUNTIE #6

Auntie's knitting a baby inside her
And sometimes it gives her a kick;
When it gets out and sees those hats
It'll give her another one quick.

JEREMY'S HOUSE

Jeremy hasn't a roof on his house
For he likes to look at the stars;
When he lies in his bed
With them all overhead
He imagines that he can see Mars.

Sometimes a thunderstorm lights up the sky
And Jeremy gets soaking wet;
But he says that it's worth it
To lie in his bed
And see folks go past in a jet.

He's counting the stars in the Milky Way,
It's going to take him forever;
But Jeremy's patiently
Counting away
For he knows it's a worthwhile endeavour.

CAREFUL CONNIE

Careful Connie's terrified
Of accidents and ills,
Of gyms and germs and things that squirm,
Heights and depths and heat and chills;
Of bicycles and buses,
Cats and cows and lakes and hills,
Flying things and furry things;

So Careful Connie never will . . .

Climb a tree	might fall down
Go swimming	might drown
Play in the rain	might get muddy
Play games	might get bloody
Cross the street	might get hit
Pet a dog	might get bit
Eat candy	might get a toothache
Eat pizza	might get a bellyache
Read a book	might ruin her eyes
Say hello	might have to say goodbye

Careful Connie's oh, so carefully
Sitting in her room,
She's absolutely safe there,
Just sitting in the gloom.
She never laughs and never cries,
She never falls and bumps her head,
She's going to live forever
But she might as well be . . . .

SPELLING

Teacher says I don't spell very well,
She says I mite even fail;
If I do I'll cry
I mite even dy
And that's the end of my tail.

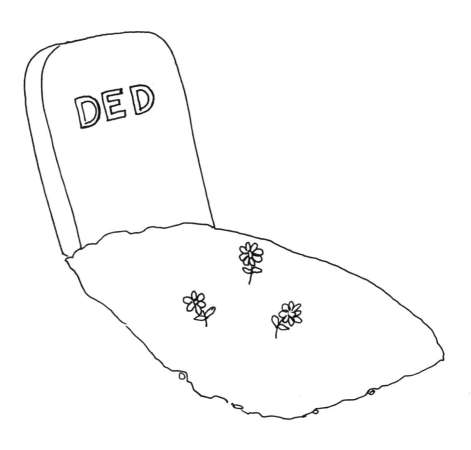

ARITHMETIC TEST

My hand is sweaty + it's hard to write,
My sweater's itchy + I'm all uptight;
I got the feeling I'm under arrest,
I'm writing another arithmetic test.

I'm clamped to my pencil + my mind's gone blank,
My dad is the manager of the bank;
Bonnie is bent over, writing away,
I used to like Bonnie. Yesterday.

Oh, why did I wear this prickly sweater?
+ why are my brains all glued together?
I studied a little but now I forget.
I wish I could fall on a bayonet.

I count 9x7 on my fingers + thumbs
But I get mixed up + my mind's gone numb;
Bonnie is finished with her hand in the air,
I'm starting to itch in my underwear.

It's Grandma's birthday. She's 63.
That's it! That's it! 9x7, gee!
The next one's easy, the next one, too,
My brains are starting to unglue.

The answers are in there, well, some of them are,
Except 9x8 + 9x4
+ 8x9 + my bum is numb,
There goes the bell + I'm nowhere near done.

Bonnie is saying "wasn't that easy?"
My throat is dry + my stomach's squeezy;
Bonnie is saying "wasn't that cinchy?"
My feet are cold + my head feels pinchy.

I sit outside by the schoolhouse wall
+ I don't play jacks + I don't play ball;
Dad will say "well, how's the math hater?"
As he adds up his bills on the calculator.

I'm feeling so bad I just wish I could die
+ have a nice funeral + everyone cry
+ never, *never* sit at my desk
Writing another arithmetic test.

AUNTIE #7

Auntie's knitting baby booties
That fit my little finger;
If Auntie's baby fits those boots
It won't have long to linger.

TRIP TO THE SEASHORE

We drove to the seashore,
My ma and pa,
Brother Bertie
And Sue and me;
From Biggar, Saskatchewan,
Over the mountains,
What did we see?
We saw the sea.

Sister Sue said
"Isn't it big?
It's bigger than Biggar
Or anything yet."
Brother Bertie
Up to his knees,
And Ma to her ankles
Said "Isn't it wet?"

I let out a yelp
When I saw kelp
And a scuttling crab,
Pa laughed at that;
He sat on the land
With his toes in the sand,
"I'll be darned," he said,
"Isn't it flat?"

At the seafood restaurant
Ma had oysters,
They looked horrid,
Green and squishy;

There were boats through the window,
Sue had scallops,
(Pa said we had to have
Something fishy).

Bertie had lobster,
I had crab,
We looked through the window
At waves and foam;
Pa had whisky
And fish and chips,
He said, "We've seen it,
Let's go home."

We drove all day
We travelled all night,
The parents and Sue
And Bertie and I;
We fought over comics
And seashells and Pa yelled
"Look at the mountains!
Aren't they high?"

We got home to Biggar,
Ma and Pa,
Sister Sue
And Bertie and me;
Pa said "Look,
Isn't it beautiful?
Big and flat,
Just like the sea."

SIR HENRY BORING

Sir Henry Boring is always exploring
Tall mountains and jungles and prairies;
"Ho hum," yawns he,
"It's plain to see,
This is all very ordinary."

Sir Henry has glanced, quite unentranced,
At scenes from Qu'Appelle to Trieste;
But no matter how pretty
The country or city,
Sir Henry remains unimpressed.

It's plain to see he'll inevitably
Be bored from Grenada to Guelph;
If he'll sing me a song
I'll tell him what's wrong,
Sir Henry is taking *himself* along,
Sir Henry is taking himself.

AUNTIE #8

Auntie's knitting the baby a suit
With a maple leaf, all white and red;
If they don't have a flag on Canada Day
They can fly the baby instead.

WALKING
(for Betty)

There goes Betty Binns
Walking in her sleep;
Down the stairs, across the floor,
Down the hall and out the door,
Along the walk and through the gate,
Walking in her sleep.

There goes Betty Binns
Talking in her sleep;
She says hello to Mrs. Brown,
To Mr. Brown and Miss Brown,
"Hello, hello," to all the Browns,
Talking in her sleep.

There goes Betty Binns
Walking in her sleep;
Up one street and down the other
Followed by her anxious mother,
(They told her not to stop her daughter
Walking in her sleep).

There goes Betty Binns
Walking in her sleep;
And Mr. Binns and Mrs. Binns
(With slippers on and hair in pins)
And Loey Binns and Teddy Binns
Walking after Betty Binns
Walking in her sleep.

BUBBLES

My mom takes the prettiest bubble baths
With the bubbles piled up, oh, so high;
All full of rainbows and fluffy white foam,
Like billowing clouds in the sky.

Sometimes we have one together
And we laugh in the bubbly water;
Oh, when my mother takes *me* in the tub
It's just lovely being her daughter!

We pile up the bubbles on top of our heads,
We hang them like beards from our chins;
We pat them on elbows and shoulders and backs
Like soft white feathery fins.

We make webs between our fingers,
Bubbly bows for our hair;
When me and my mom take a bubble bath,
We hardly leave anything bare.

PRISM

There's a prism in our window
That makes rainbows on the wall;
There's another in the bathroom
Making rainbows in the hall.

There's a prism in my bedroom
Throwing rainbows on my bed;
If I had one in my eye
I'd have rainbows in my head.

HOW DO YOU SAY GOODBYE?

How do you say goodbye to a house
When you're moving forever on Saturday,
When you've lived there always — seven years,
And no matter what, they won't let you stay.

How do you say goodbye to a room
With its just-right walls and corners and nooks;
With its Snoopy curtains, all faded and blue,
And shelves for your toys, and fishtank, and books.

How do you say goodbye to the tree
That grew up so tall by your bedroom window,
That dances its leaves on your yellow walls
And lulls you to sleep whenever the wind blows.

How do you say goodbye to a street
Where you know all the hedges and places to hide,
The back alley fence where you broke your arm,
And the hill at the end where you used to slide?

I wish I could move this house and this tree —
This yard — this street — these swings;
My friends can all come and visit me,
But how do you say goodbye to *things*?

AUNTIE #9

Auntie's baby arrived last night
In a regular shape and size;
Now it doesn't have a single hat
In which to socialize.

AUNTIE #10

Auntie's baby is ever so sweet,
Soft and round and cuddly;
With two little eyes like raisins,
Just like Uncle Dudley.

AUNTIE #11

Auntie's baby is starting to talk,
He's quite a bright little critter;
The first words little Dudley said
Were "Mama's a *terrible* knitter."

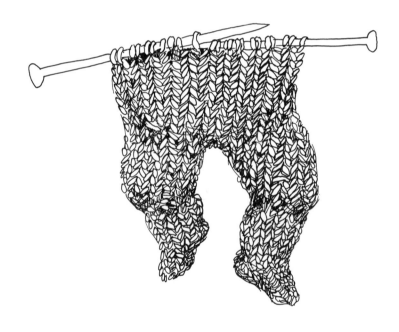